LE JAPON ARTISTIQUE

LE JAPON
ARTISTIQUE

Japanese Floral Pattern Design in the Art Nouveau Era

From the Collection of the Museum of Fine Arts, Boston

Introduction by Rachel Saunders

CHRONICLE BOOKS
SAN FRANCISCO

BOSTON

Library of Congress Cataloging-in-Publication Data available.

ISBN: 978-0-8118-7276-8

Manufactured in China

Designed by Andrew Schapiro

10 9 8 7 6 5 4 3 2 1

Chronicle Books LLC
680 Second Street
San Francisco, CA 94107
www.chroniclebooks.com

Contents

NEW ART FOR OLD

Art Nouveau and Early Twentieth Century Japanese Design Books

JAPAN,

like Europe, has a long history of using design pattern books. Prior to the generalized spread of woodblock printing technology, manuscript compilations of patterns for use in textiles or model books for carpenters, for example, were carefully recorded, guarded, and transmitted within specialist artisan family lineages. In the mid-seventeenth century, Japan experienced a publishing boom that resulted in a veritable explosion, first in the production of woodblock printed books, followed from the mid-1760s on by full-color single-sheet prints of beauties and actors. These prints were the ukiyo-e or "pictures of the floating world" that were later to capture the imaginations of painters such as Monet and van Gogh half a world away in Europe.

The segregated licensed pleasure quarters of the capital, in which the "floating world" was both geographically and psychologically located, were places of escape from the strictly ordered Neo-Confucian society of early modern Japan. Real-world concerns and identities were to be left at the gates, and their essence was very much to be taken in the moment. In such places where high-class courtesans and entertainers enjoyed what we would think of today as celebrity status, fashion was of great importance. In 1666, relatively early in the book boom, we find a publisher taking a gamble on that fascination for fashion and publishing the first printed kimono pattern book (Fig. 1). This little book,

FIGURE I

of which only one copy of the first printing is now known to exist, signals a significant change in the concept of the design book. Kimono pattern books such as this were not simply published in multiple copies so that they could be used by customers to select designs for their kimonos. They were produced much as magazines are today, for consumption and for pleasure. Some, like this book, included literary puzzles and puns hidden in the patterns, requiring readers to be visually as well as verbally literate to catch the full appeal of the urbane designs.

Kimono pattern books were followed by other kinds of printed design books. The painter Ōoka Shunboku (1680–1763), known for his multivolume anthologies of canonical paintings, produced a beautiful book of architectural designs entitled *Ranma zushiki* [Designs for Decorative Transoms] in 1734 (Fig. 2). Katsushika Hokusai (1760–1849), one of the most familiar of all Japanese artists in the West, also produced exquisite books of designs for ornamental hair combs and smoking pipes. Kimono fashions, of course, changed with the times, and by the early nineteenth century, when smaller all-over patterns were favored, it was no longer really necessary from a practical point of view to render a full-body image of a kimono to understand how a kimono would look. But the pattern books continued to be published well into the nineteenth century, as older

FIGURE 2.1

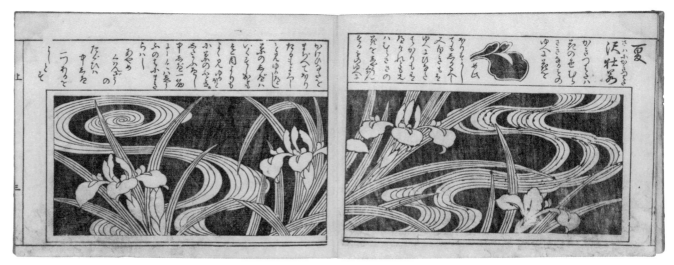

FIGURE 2.2

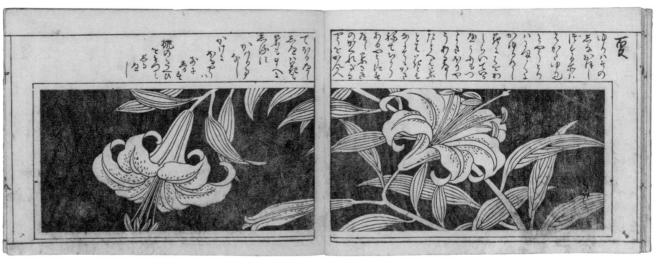

books containing styles of the past were reprinted, signaling an established market for the appreciation of pattern books as a genre.

Beginning in the last decade of the nineteenth century, and especially in the years immediately following 1900, design books of a slightly different kind began to be published by the Kyoto publisher Unsōdō. Despite the availability of less labor-intensive means of reproduction by this time, Unsōdō produced its books in the traditional way, commissioning carvers to produce woodblocks, which were then inked and printed by hand. The resulting books are outstanding examples of fine printing, and the publisher continues to preserve the technical and design excellence rooted in traditional Japanese woodblock printing in its publications today. A number of the early twentieth century design books were printed with multiple design "swatches" of repeatable patterns in smaller formats with practical reference for designers in mind. Others, though, are examples of virtuoso design clearly produced for more general consumption. The images reproduced here from two such books—*Chigusa* [A Thousand Grasses], which was first published 1899–1900, designed by Kamisaka Sekka (1866–1942); and *Shasei sōka moyō* [Patterns of Flowers and Grasses from Life], 1907, designed by Furuya Kōrin (1875–1910)—belong to the latter category. Both books feature bold designs based on plants and flowers that traverse space on the page in contrasting yet equally considered ways.

On first examination, the use of conspicuously considered color planes and sinuous line are highly suggestive of the decorative Art Nouveau style, most actively practiced in Europe in the short period between about 1895 and 1905. Certainly there are superficial similarities, but these are counterbalanced by the linearity of the asymmetrical background planes that cut through the graceful curves of the flower forms, the drama of the distinctive color schemes, even the selection of plants. But just how Art Nouveau are these creations?

The Art Nouveau style is characterized by organic designs based overwhelmingly on plants and flowers, which are patternized often through the flattening of forms into color planes defined by the use of strong outline, and its hallmark "whiplash" curved lines. In its original conception, the emphasis was on the creation of entire decorative schemes and the style was applied to the decorative arts and architecture, bringing art into the design of daily life in unified artistic environments. Strongly influenced by and, in turn, nurtured in the work of artists and architects including Alphonse Mucha (1860–1939), Eugène Grasset (1841–1917), Victor Horta (1861–1947), Louis Comfort Tiffany (1848–1933), and Emile Gallé (1846–1904), the style was propelled by the Parisian art dealer Siegfried Bing from 1895, when he opened his gallery, L'Art Nouveau, at 22 Rue de Provence, and reached its zenith at the 1900 Paris Exposition Universelle.

Bing was an early enthusiast of Japanese art and skillfully navigated the wave of Japonisme, the mania for all things Japanese, which began to sweep across Europe following the opening of Japan to the West in 1854 after more than two hundred years of effective political and economic isolation. Bing himself travelled to Japan in 1880, and he dealt with many of the most prominent collectors of Japanese art in Europe and the United States. In 1888 he established a journal called *Le Japon Artistique*, and in the first issue described Japanese art as an "art nouveau," predicting that it would have a profound impact on European art. Bing was, of course, not the first to observe the "new," or more accurately, the unfamiliar in Japanese art. Japanese ukiyo-e prints with their use of cropped perspective, black ink outlines, and strong color planes, as well as their perceived sensitivity to highly specific atmospheric conditions and times of day, had already caught the attention of Edouard Manet (1832–1883), Edgar Dégas (1834–1917), and the early Impressionists. Bing's concern, though, was less with painting and more with the re-enlivenment of French design and the applied arts.

With the inception in 1851 of the era of World's Fairs, at which nations displayed their cultural and commercial products competitively, it had become clear to some that French design had become complacent and stagnant, its evolution hampered by the constraints of formal academic painting, symbolism, and the weight of history in which the fine arts were grounded. Bing's "nouveau" lay in the unencumbered freshness he saw in Japanese art, and in the flexibility and fertility he recognized in the perceived lack of distinction between the fine and decorative arts in Japan.

Although it is most often ukiyo-e prints that are cited as having had a revolutionary effect on European visual creativity, in fact distinctive flattened color planes; organic, calligraphically inflected line; and an unfamiliar and striking sense of compositional space were also to be found in the spectacular paintings of the so-called Rinpa school, which found an altogether different register of praise in Paris. "Rinpa" is a posthumous name for a loose affiliation of artists, named for one of the earliest exponents of the style, Ogata Kōrin (1658–1716). Kōrin, a native of the old capital of Kyoto, developed a style in which he excerpted and enlarged literary motifs taken from classical Japanese painting rooted in a courtly aesthetic. Significantly, Kōrin was working at a time when real political power had recently been removed from the imperial court in Kyoto by a military shogun, who had established a new capital in the eastern city of Edo (present-day Tokyo).

FIGURE 3.1

FIGURE 3.2

As they were effectively held captive in the shells of their own disempowered status, calligraphy on highly decorated papers and paintings redolent of a classical golden age of courtly supremacy found favor among aristocrats and those of means in Kyoto. The use of gold and silver, in particular as backgrounds for screen paintings, and strong emphasis on the depiction of seasonal flowers and grasses, themselves loaded with centuries-old poetic valence, characterize the Rinpa "style." The motifs thrum with a curious tension between the illusion of detailed, realistic depiction highly evocative of actual forms, and abstraction in form and composition. This is most clearly visible in the way painting subjects hover above flat metallic backgrounds, as in Figure 3, where the poppies grow in entirely convincing natural formations out of an impossible gold earth.

The transmission of the Rinpa style occurred rather loosely since it was not an established professional painting school with an associated workshop apparatus. Artists associated themselves with the line by copying the works of earlier masters as homage, but also as a way of bringing new life to the style, and they would often change their names to signal their self-declared membership of the line. With the spread of woodblock printing, paintings by the early masters were anthologized in books such as *Kōrin gafu* [The Kōrin Picture Album] by Nakamura Hōchū, first published in 1826 (see pages 29–35);

Ōson gafu [The Ōson Picture Album] by Sakai Hōitsu, first published in 1817 (see pages 37–45); and *Kōrin hyakuzu* [One Hundred Designs by Kōrin], 1815. The very process of selection, abbreviation, and gradual stylization in the preparation of these books in many ways prepared the way for their later applications in design.

Whether or not Western collectors appreciated Rinpa painting with a full awareness of the often melancholy intellectual evocation of the classical Japanese poetry and literature that had originally animated it, a number were clearly highly enthusiastic about its aesthetic merits. The art historian Louis Gonse (1846–1921) writing in 1890, declared: "Kōrin! I like the name, the turn of it, and the rhythm. It undulates, trails along, and has an air of antiquity about it which practically amounts to a picture. . . . Kōrin is the first rank of those who have carried to the highest pitch the intuition and genius of decoration."[1] The judicious use of inflected line, powerful application of color, and compositional devices such as flattening of form and undulating lateral distribution of motifs, if not the original intellectual and literary content of Rinpa painting, are clearly present in Art Nouveau design.

While the Art Nouveau style may be widely popular today, it was met with considerable critical hostility in turn-of-the-century France. Initial Japanese reactions were also less than entirely favorable. The painter Asai

Chū (1856–1907), who visited the 1900 Exposition Universelle in Paris, was more than a little taken aback by the degree to which the Art Nouveau artists had incorporated Asian art into their work. The painter and multifaceted print and craft designer Kamisaka Sekka, who encountered the "New Art" in Glasgow in 1901, reacted more strongly, hotly denying its newness by arguing that its very principles had been in use in classical Japanese painting for centuries. Sekka in particular seems to have caught the scent of Japonisme on Art Nouveau. The moment was a sensitive one: Japan had only recently emerged onto the world stage as a nation state. Driven largely by the desire to avoid the colonization by Western nations witnessed in other parts of East Asia, a full-scale campaign of national self-definition and modernization, which in many ways looked like Westernization, was underway in Japan. Within this context, the World's Fairs provided a conspicuous and charged stage for the display of national identity, and in Japan the matter of which objects were to be displayed took on documentable dimensions of national significance.

Following the West's initial enthusiasm for Japanese exotica, wares produced for export had attempted to pander to the Japanese perception of the kinds of goods Westerners favored, resulting in self-exoticized works that were ultimately economically unsuccessful. In an attempt to boost the general level of domestic design in order to counteract the causes of the fall-off in trade in export wares, a Design Bureau was established under the aegis of the Ministry of the Interior, and designs for objects sent to the World's Fairs in the late 1870s and early 1880s were collated and circulated to artisans all over Japan. These compilations were titled *Onchi zuroku*, reflecting the maxim *onko chishi*, "honor the ancient and replenish it with the new." The realization that Westerners were more interested in Japan's antiquities than its contemporary export wares was given particular specificity in 1884, when a Japanese arts administrator practically called Louis Comfort Tiffany a thief for his application of Japan's classical art to his own designs.[2] It was clearly recognized that no economic benefit would accrue to Japan, the country of origin, from *this* kind of outflow of artistic capital.

Though neither Asai Chū nor Kamisaka Sekka endorsed the Art Nouveau style, it certainly caused both to reconsider the state of Japan's own contemporary design world as a matter of urgency. When Asai returned from Europe to Kyoto in 1902, he took up a position as professor of design at the newly established *Kyōto Kōtō Kōgei Gakkō* [Kyoto Higher School of Crafts], the mission of which was to bring reform through education to "conservative" Japanese design. Asai worked with the architect Takeda Goichi (1872–1938), to implement a new design education curriculum, which included teaching

design and design principles from European design books they may even have carried to Japan themselves, including Maurice Pillard Verneuil's *L'Animal dans la Décoration* (1890) and Eugène Grasset's seminal 1896 publication, *La Plante et ses Applications Ornamentales*. The latter was simultaneously published in English as *Plants and Their Application to Ornament*, and was republished in facsimile from the copy in the collection of the Museum of Fine Arts, Boston in 2008 (Fig. 4).

Grasset himself taught design at the École Normale d'Enseignement du Dessin in Paris, and *Plants and Their Application* is a full demonstration of his basic principles of design, which are explained briefly in his foreword. He forbids mere mimicry, saying that after first carefully studying the work of masters of the past, students should next study natural forms, followed by study of the limitations imposed by "art principles" upon natural forms when the designer comes to employ them pictorially and in ornamentation. Each flower selected for use in Grasset's book has three pages devoted to it: the first a naturalistic exploration of the flower or plant from various angles, the following two composed of patternized, ornamental applications for wallpaper, textiles, and tiles derived from the plant. "An artisan is above all one who has learnt the nature of the vehicle he works in," Grasset declares.

Grasset was a close associate of the Parisian printer Charles Gillot (1853–1903). Gillot printed Grasset's work, and Grasset masterminded the interior decoration for Gillot's new home in 1879. Gillot's son was also Grasset's pupil for several years. Gillot was a well-known collector of Japanese art, and when part of his enormous collection was sold in 1904, it required a two-volume catalogue, graced with plates. He collected a wider range of Japanese arts than was usual for his time, though ukiyo-e prints, the most common focus of attention, were also numerically well represented. The catalogue also lists a few Rinpa paintings and a number of Rinpa-related woodblock printed books, including *A Hundred Designs by Kōrin*, and *Shinsen Kōrin hyakuzu* [New Selection of One Hundred Designs by Kōrin], 1864, as well as a copy of Ōoka Shunboku's book of architectural designs, *Designs for Decorative Transoms* (Fig. 2), allowing the interesting possibility that Grasset may have viewed and been influenced by these very works.

The scholar Christophe Marquet believes it is quite possible that Asai Chū, the painter who appears to have brought a significant culmination of that creative infusion in the form of Grasset's book to Japan, and then used it as the very textbook from which to expound design principles to renew Japanese design education, may even have met Grasset in person in Paris.[3] Whatever the exact facts of the case, it illustrates well the fluidity and circularity of the situation, and indicates that even in this early stage of the development of modern art, conceptual designations such as "East" and "West" vastly oversimplify the oscillations between cultural spheres taking place on the ground.

Kamisaka Sekka, who had so objected to Art Nouveau in Glasgow, had espoused the historically charged Rinpa style even before setting out for Europe. On his return to Japan in 1902, he produced a string of woodblock printed design books with the publisher Unsōdō. These books—including *Kairo* [The Sea Route], 1902; *Chō senshu* [A Thousand Butterflies], 1904; and most famously *Momoyogusa* [A World of Things], 1909–1910—reflect an intense focus on the essential source material of Art Nouveau, Japanese Rinpa painting, and Sekka's careful consideration of how this native, self-consciously classical school of painting could be used to inspire newly enlivened, high-quality design in Japan from first principles. Sekka was working in the same circles as Asai Chū, and the Kyoto design world underwent a marked transformation in the early 1900s largely as a result of their efforts. Their "re-importation" of Ogata Kōrin sparked a "Kōrin boom" in Kyoto, which in fact outlasted the short-lived Art Nouveau in Europe. The craze for beautifully crafted Kōrin-esque designs that employed masterfully choreographed abstracted classical motifs developed along slightly different lines in Tokyo in kimono designs produced for the Mitsukoshi Department Store.

Sekka's *A Thousand Grasses* was first published in 1899, just prior to his trip to Europe. The flowering plants reproduced here are enlarged and presented in cropped perspective so that we are left with a sense of heightened proximity. In line with Rinpa norms, the flowers are depicted with convincing attention to naturalistic form, and all are readily identifiable. But in these prints, Sekka also pushes the familiar tension between realism and abstraction further than the paintings of his predecessors. These flowers are only present by their absence: they are inverted, left unprinted, and their forms are delineated only by the colors of the background planes out of which they emerge.

Still not content, Sekka pushes the possibilities of design even further by dividing the ground into asymmetric bands of carefully selected colors that abut each other with uncompromising linearity. The plants sweep elegantly over these geometric boundary lines. Logically, since they appear as "cut-outs" on areas of the paper left unprinted, they should appear recessed. But, in fact precisely because they cross these boundary lines, the flowers float well above the ground, recalling the techniques of earlier Rinpa painting masters. In so explicitly foregrounding the construction of these images, Sekka makes it difficult for the viewer to ignore the mechanics of the composition—his rendering presence by absence, his pushing and pulling within the planes of the image itself, as well as within the historically self-inscriptive Rinpa style in which he had chosen to work—mean that the images articulate their status as "design" to the viewer as much as they present the careful study and thorough understanding "from life" of Rinpa painting itself.

Although no direct evidence has yet been uncovered to suggest Sekka was working with reference to Western photographic images, there is a strong visual resonance in these images from *A Thousand Grasses* with those produced by the early English photographer Anna Atkins (1799–1871), who placed real plants on photographic paper and then exposed them to produce photograms like the one in Figure 5. Her remarkable part-book *Photographs of British Algae: Cyanotype Images*, begun in 1843, the first book in the world to be produced using photography, was conceived as a complement to another scientific manual on algae. Atkins was led to the photographic technique after despairing of the usual methods of illustration for capturing the likeness of such intricate plants. Despite the scientific underpinnings of the work, Atkins clearly exercised her highly developed aesthetic judgment in arranging the plants she photographed. Her photograms have an ethereal three-dimensional depth to them, but the tension between abstraction and realism is even more exquisitely poised than in Sekka's designs precisely because the inverted shadow image of the plant *is* the very plant itself.

FIGURE 5

In *Patterns of Flowers and Grasses from Life,* Furuya Kōrin presses the design questions Sekka raises in *A Thousand Grasses* still further. Kōrin, who was born Fuji Tarō in 1875, marked himself as a follower of the Rinpa school by changing his name in the time-honored fashion. He moved to Kyoto as a student, and after studying Chinese and Japanese literature, apprenticed in the Kyoto-based Shijō painting school, and then to Kamisaka Sekka, from whom he learned drawing and design. In 1905 he was made assistant professor at the *Kyōto Shiritsu Bijutsu Kōgei Gakkō* (Kyoto Municipal School of Arts and Crafts). Kōrin was not only educated in painting and design, he also took instruction in architecture, and charcoal drawing lessons from Asai Chū, who by this time was teaching design at the Kyoto Higher School of Crafts. He was extremely active in the early twentieth century Kyoto design scene, participating in multiple exhibitions and competitions. He produced eleven design books between 1902 and 1908 with the publisher Unsōdō, one in collaboration with Sekka, and would no doubt have produced more had his life not been cut tragically short by illness in 1910.

Patterns of Flowers and Grasses from Life is his finest book, and is clearly intended more as a book for contemplation and appreciation than as a design primer. The book's title is printed on the cover as if handwritten on the top sheet of a pile of colored papers, carefully arranged so that just their layered edges are revealed. This may be a glancing reference to the practice of decorating calligraphy papers through collage, or color-coordinating the shades of the many layers of a kimono so that they peep out at the sleeves in a tasteful cascade, both aesthetic practices associated with the classical, courtly golden age of the Heian period (794–1185). Its self-conscious framing, though, hardly prepares the viewer for the contents. The thoroughly modern designs are compelling, but they are scarcely comfortable in the way that Sekka's harmoniously coordinated, pastel-toned designs are. Kōrin's palette is both bolder and more experimental, and many of his flower forms are noticeably worm-eaten or beginning to wilt. Stylistically we may recognize Art Nouveau-esque curving tendrils and whiplash lines, see the influence of the Vienna Secessionists here and there, or feel a flash of affinity between some of the gentler designs and Liberty-designed fabrics. But the dissonance between the dynamism of his designs and the suspended decay in the leaves of his flowering plants rhythmically punctuates the viewing experience, generating a feeling of sometimes having been brought perhaps a little too close for comfort to these plants.

Like Sekka, Kōrin returns to essentials and reinvestigates Rinpa painting techniques and motifs in his designs. This is most obvious in his use of metallic pigments, and in the use of particular floral motifs, such as the iris, which was favored in Rinpa painting not only for its beauty, but also for its poetic valence. Kōrin also complexifies Sekka's use of multiple color planes as ground for his flowers, proportionally increasing the kineticism of his designs. In some cases, the effect seems to evoke the experience of viewing painted flowers as light hits the angled panels of a folding screen, similar to the one shown in Figure 3. But Kōrin does not stop his explorations there, investigating the possibilities of the Shijō painting school in the designs produced without outline. There also appear to be strong resonances with the work of two master artists in particular, Shibata Zeshin (1807–1891) and the eccentric Kyoto painter Itō Jakuchū (1716–1800). The work of both of these artists was featured at the World's Fairs; a whole "Jakuchū Room" was even created for the Louisiana Purchase International Exposition, St. Louis, in 1904.

Jakuchū is best known for his large-scale paintings of birds and flowers, which also powerfully manipulate the tension between realism and abstraction, as the hyper-real feathers of his birds and the blossoms of his flowers spread to cover the entire ground, in the process devolving into pattern. It is possible Kōrin may have been able to see Jakuchū's work in person in Kyoto. Unsōdō's publication in 1908 of a printed book of Jakuchū ceiling paintings for a Kyoto temple, and the reproduction in 1909 of two woodblock printed books designed by Jakuchū in 1768, brings the two artists together under Unsōdō's umbrella. Jakuchū's 1768 books, titled *Genpo yōka* [Jade Blossoms of Mount Kunlun] and *Sokenjō* [Soken Model], contain a series of remarkable images of flowering plants and insects that are rendered in imitation of rubbings, so that the bulk of the page is inked black, and the images appear in reserve. The leaves of all the plants are conspicuously bug-eaten, and there are unmistakable echoes in Kōrin's designs of the dramatic way in which Jakuchū's plants swoop and curve to fill the compositional space, as well as in the very plants selected. Though Unsōdō's republication of Jakuchū's books took place shortly after the publication of *Patterns of Flowers and Grasses from Life*, it seems likely, given the circles in which he was working, that Kōrin was aware of these works.

For the same reasons, it seems equally unlikely that Kōrin did not know Grasset's *Plants and Their Application to Ornament*. In the preface to *Flowers and Grasses from Life*, Kōrin writes that his book is the result of his own obsessive compilation of many examples of floral designs, and that he hopes it may serve as something of a corrective since the many "from life" patterns published in recent times all seem to tend toward one specific application or another. Kōrin's self-deprecating hope is that his designs might be applied in various situations, making a useful contribution to the design world. While Grasset's book certainly does provide specific pattern models for specific uses, its wider significance is in its demonstration of design principles— drawing from life, patternizing successfully from the understanding that drawing from life provides, and then applying the resulting ornamental patterns. Kōrin's designs, rooted in a thorough understanding of the artistic styles with which he worked, in particular Rinpa painting, are remarkable examples of design in which the natural forms are patternized so that they both traverse and define space. The final stage of the process, the application, Kōrin says he is leaving open for his viewers, which also allows them to simply enjoy the prints as they stand if they so desire.

The prints reproduced here were made for appreciation, but they are also prints that explicitly employ design principles, imported from Europe through the medium of Japan's own painting traditions, which were then carefully re-transmuted, re-enlivened, and published by artists and a publishing house both clearly committed to contemporary Japanese design. The re-importation process via Art Nouveau, and the shock to the system it occasioned, resulted in design motifs being invested with greater texture, as designers such as Furuya Kōrin broadened the reach of their source materials. Produced in a Japanese cultural context, it is more than tempting to read back into Kōrin's images some of the historical and symbolic content that Bing and others rather ironically saw Japanese art as being so blissfully unburdened by. Kōrin's design of a flowering gourd (*yūgao*, or evening face) before a silver moon (page 84), for example, might well have been read with the so-called "Evening Faces" chapter of the early eleventh century novel *The Tale of Genji* in mind, in which a beautiful young woman is tragically killed by a jealous spirit. Equally, the iris motif (page 80) signals a famous poem on separation from the ninth-century Japanese classic *Tales of Ise*. While reading the images this way may add an extra dimension to their enjoyment, it is certainly not necessary, for these aesthetically arresting, beautifully crafted designs stand not only as witness to the potency of international artistic exchange of the turn of the nineteenth century, but more importantly, as testament to the enduring appeal of successful design, which remains as relevant today as in the day of their creation.

For complete image credits, please see page 123–125.

[1] Cited in Clark, Timothy. "The Intuition and the Genius of Decoration," in Yamane Yūzō et al., *Rimpa Art from the Idemitsu Collection, Tokyo*, London, British Museum Press, 1998, p. 68

[2] Cited in Foxwell, Chelsea. "Japan as Museum? Encapsulating Change and Loss in Late-Nineteenth-Century Japan," *Getty Research Journal*, Number 1, 2009, p. 45

[3] Marquet, Christophe. "Paris no Asai Chū—zuan e no mezame," *Kindai gasetsu: Meiji Bijutsu Gakkaishi*, No. 1, 1992, pp. 19–26

KŌRIN GAFU

–Nakamura Hōchū

Published in 1802

ŌSON GAFU

–Sakai Hōitsu

Published in 1 8 1 7

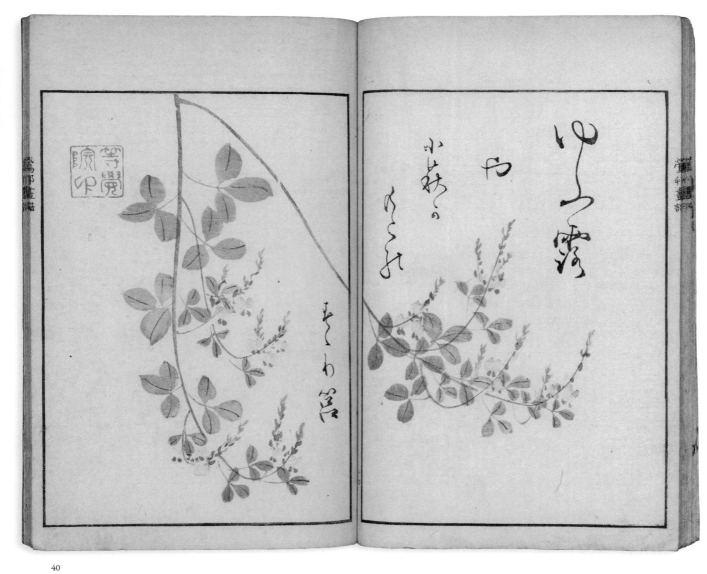

CHIGUSA

–Kamisaka Sekka

Published in 1905

SHASEI SŌKA MOYŌ

–Furuya Kōrin

Published in 1907

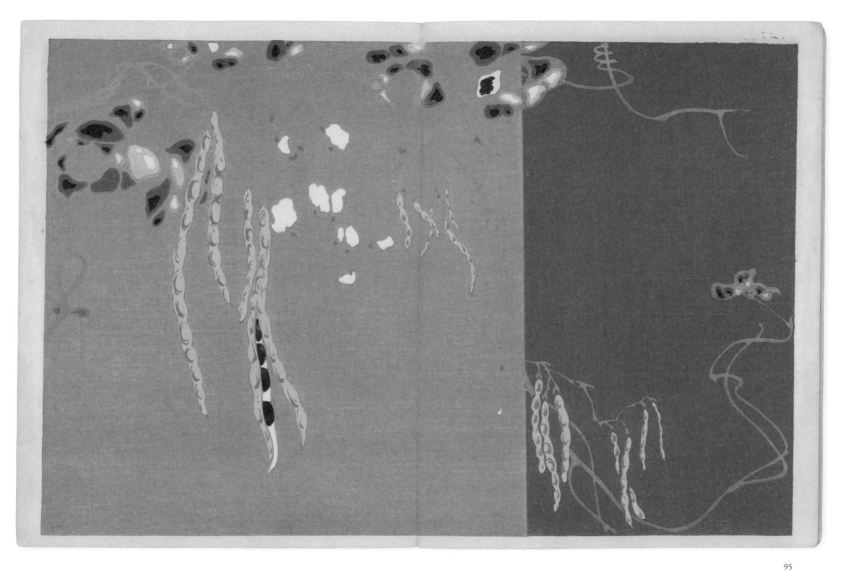

LEONARD A. LAUDER COLLECTION OF JAPANESE POSTCARDS

Mid-Nineteenth Century

太陽附録繪端書
（博文館發行）

僕ちよっと知らんうちに
一寸僻行ったてすゐ
電話ですべゝたが

神戸市兵庫
西尾池村苅藻通
一ノ二六

その返よぴーゐ
右

九月ア

すゝゑ

Image Credits

Page 14, Figure 1
Artist: Unknown, Japanese
Publisher: Yamada Ichirōbei
Title: *Shinsen on-hiinagata* [A New Selection of Respected Patterns]
Date: Edo period, 1666 (Kanbun 6)
Medium: Woodblock printed book; ink on paper
Dimensions: 18.2 x 23.0 cm (*kohon*)
Museum of Fine Arts, Boston
Source unidentified, 2000.1258

Page 15, Figures 2.1 and 2.2
Artist: Ōoka Shunboku, Japanese, 1680–1763
Publishers: Suhara Mohei (Edo) and Onogi Ichibei (Osaka)
Title: *Ranma zushiki* [Designs for Decorative Transoms]
Date: Edo period, about 1734 (Kyōhō 19)
Medium: Woodblock printed book; ink on paper
Dimensions: 19.4 x 26.3 cm (*yokobon*)
Museum of Fine Arts, Boston
Gift of Mrs. Jared K. Morse in memory of Charles J. Morse,
2007.52.1-3

Page 18, Figures 3.1 and 3.2
School of: Tawaraya Sōtatsu, Japanese, died about 1642
Title: *Poppies*
Date: Edo period, 17th century
Medium: Pair of six-panel folding screens; ink, color, and gold leaf on paper
Dimensions: 150.3 x 352.8 cm
Museum of Fine Arts, Boston
Gift of Mrs. W. Scott Fitz, 11.1272-3

Page 21, Figures 4.1, 4.2, and 4.3
Artist: Maurice Pillard Verneuil, French, 1869–1942
Publisher: Chapman & Hall, Ltd (London)
Title: *Iris,* plates 1–3 from Eugène Grasset, *Plants and Their Application to Ornament*
Date: 1897
Medium: Color lithographs
Dimensions: 45.6 x 33.6 x 3.8 cm
Museum of Fine Arts, Boston
Gift of Ann Vershbow and Charles Beitz, 2004.2272

Page 24, Figure 5
Artist: Anna Atkins, English, 1799–1871
Title: *Thistle (Carduus acanthoides)*
Date: 1851–1854
Medium: Photograph, photogram (cyanotype)
Dimensions: 34.9 x 24.8 cm
Museum of Fine Arts, Boston
Sophie M. Friedman Fund, 1986.593

BOOKS

Pages 31–35
Artist: Nakamura Hōchū, Japanese, active about 1799–1818
Author of preface: Tachibana Chikage, 1735–1808
Publisher: Izumiya Shōjirō (Edo)
Title: *Kōrin gafu* [The Kōrin Picture Album]
Date: Edo period, first published 1802; this edition 1826 (Bunsei 9)
Medium: Woodblock printed book; ink and color on paper
Dimensions: 27.7 x 18.9 cm (*ōhon*)
Museum of Fine Arts, Boston
Gift of Mrs. Jared K. Morse in memory of Charles J. Morse, 1997.533.1-2

Pages 39–45
Artist: Sakai Hōitsu, Japanese, 1761–1828
Author of preface: Kamo Suetaka
Publisher: Izumiya Shōjirō (Edo)
Title: *Ōson gafu* [The Ōson Picture Album]
Date: Edo period, 1817 (Bunka 14)
Medium: Woodblock printed book; ink and color on paper
Dimensions: 27.8 x 18.8 cm (*ōhon*)
Museum of Fine Arts, Boston
Gift of Mrs. Jared K. Morse in memory of Charles J. Morse, 1997.535

Pages 49–61
Artist: Kamisaka Sekka, Japanese, 1866–1942
Publisher: Unsōdō (Kyoto)
Title: *Chigusa* [Myriad Grasses] (vols. 2 and 3)
Date: Meiji era, 1905 (Meiji 38)
Medium: Woodblock printed book; ink, color, and metallic pigments on paper
Dimensions: 23.8 x 35.7 cm (*ōhon*)
Museum of Fine Arts, Boston
Kojiro Tomita, 2007.55.1-2
Reproduced with permission from UNSODO Corporation

Pages 65–114
Artist and author of preface: Furuya Kōrin, Japanese, 1875–1910
Publisher: Unsōdō (Kyoto)
Title: *Shasei sōka moyō* [Patterns of Plants and Flowers from Nature]
Date: Meiji era, 1907 (Meiji 40)
Medium: Woodblock printed book; ink, color, and metallic pigments on paper
Dimensions: 25.1 x 18.5 cm (*ōhon*)
Museum of Fine Arts, Boston
Gift of Arthur Vershbow, 2001.864.1-2
Reproduced with permission from UNSODO Corporation

POSTCARDS

Page 117
Artist Unknown, Japanese
Publisher: Hakubunkan, Japanese
Title: *Plum Tree with Wave Motifs from Taiyō*
Date: Late Meiji era
Medium: Color lithograph; ink on card stock
Dimensions: 8.8 x 13.8 cm
Museum of Fine Arts, Boston
Leonard A. Lauder Collection of Japanese Postcards, 2002.2391

Page 118
Artist Unknown, Japanese
Publisher: Nagoya Design Association (Chūkyō zuan kai)
Printed by: Aichi Prefectural School of Industry (Aichi kenritsu kōgyō gakkō)
Title: *Blossoming Plum Tree by a River*
Date: Late Meiji era
Medium: Color lithograph; ink and metallic pigment on card stock
Dimensions: 8.8 x 13.8 cm
Museum of Fine Arts, Boston
Leonard A. Lauder Collection of Japanese Postcards, 2002.1603

Page 119
Artist: Ōta Saburō, Japanese, 1884–1969
Publisher: Japanese Postcard Association (Nihon hagaki kai)
Title: *Begonia*
Date: Late Meiji era
Medium: Color lithograph; ink on card stock
Dimensions: 8.8 x 13.8 cm
Museum of Fine Arts, Boston
Leonard A. Lauder Collection of Japanese Postcards, 2002.1085

Page 120
Artist: Ōta Saburō, Japanese, 1884–1969
Publisher: Japanese Postcard Association (Nihon hagaki kai)
Distributed by: Hakubunkan
Title: *Lilies*
Date: Late Meiji era, cancelled 1908
Medium: Color lithograph; ink and metallic pigment on card stock
Dimensions: 8.8 x 13.8 cm
Museum of Fine Arts, Boston
Leonard A. Lauder Collection of Japanese Postcards, 2002.1083

Page 121
Artist Unknown, Japanese
Printed by: Aichi Prefectural School of Industry (Aichi kenritsu kōgyō gakkō)
Publisher: Nagoya Design Association (Chūkyō zuan kai)
Title: *Rising Sun and Pine Trees*
Date: Late Meiji era, cancelled 1908
Medium: Color lithograph; ink and metallic pigment on card stock
Dimensions: 8.8 x 13.8 cm
Museum of Fine Arts, Boston
Leonard A. Lauder Collection of Japanese Postcards, 2002.4383

ACKNOWLEDGMENTS

With sincere thanks to Chelsea Foxwell,
Tim Clark, Joe Earle, Nancy Keeler,
Masae Kurahashi, Anne Nishimura Morse,
Jeffrey Moser, Joan Wright, and most especially,
Arthur Vershbow. Any errors that remain
are the sole responsibility of the author.